J V Birch

ice cream 'n' tar

SurVision Books

First published in 2023 by
SurVision Books
Dublin, Ireland
Reggio di Calabria, Italy
www.survisionmagazine.com

Copyright © J V Birch, 2023

Cover image: "Melt" by Julie Cebulla
Cover image © Julie Cebulla, 2023
Design © SurVision Books, 2023

ISBN: 978-1-912963-43-0

This book is in copyright. No part of this publication may be reproduced, stored in a retrieval system, or transmitted in any form or by any means without the prior permission in writing from the publisher.

Acknowledgements

Grateful acknowledgement is made to the editors of the following, in which some of these poems, or versions of them, originally appeared:

Australian Poetry Anthology, Vol. 7 (ed. by Yvette Holt and Magan Magan; Australian Poetry Ltd., 2019): "primordial"

Ink, Sweat & Tears: "Turning"

Juniper: "Earth turn"

Kith Review: "The tap"

Mslexia: "2049"

Nightingale & Sparrow: "Crow"

Plumwood Mountain: "Coffin Bay"

The Poeming Pigeon: "Moon" and "A burning world"

Poetry for the Planet: An Anthology of Imagined Futures (ed. by Julia Kaylock and Denise O'Hagan; Litoria Press, 2021): "The Ministers"

Transnational Literature: "Ladybirds"

Writing Water: "Barrier Reef"

CONTENTS

2049	5
Moon	6
Charlie's room	7
ice cream 'n' tar	8
Snow	9
The tap	10
A burning world	11
Silver spoons	12
Earth turn	13
M. Nature Comes Home	14
Sorry	15
An Evening with the Legendary Ms. Snow	16
Ladybirds	19
Coffin Bay	20
Barrier Reef	21
Every second counts	22
Small beginnings	23
Turning	24
When the sky falls	25
Crow	26
primordial	27
The Ministers	28
After the Anthropocene	29
Epilogue: Rot	30

2049

You don't remember bees. I draw one for you,
filigree the wings in silver. Snow is something

the freezer does when you don't close the door
properly. Blue skies are daily and the moon's

lost its face. Sea levels have risen, no more
treks to the tide collecting shells. You giggle

at photos of me in tights and long sleeves.
Gloves are displayed in museums like aliens.

Ice cream shares have shot through the roof,
you ask me how many flavours I can name.

Another skin treatment's launched to make
it harder to burn (I'll never confess my sunbed

hours). Swimming is law, treading water the new
gym. You joke your kids will have webbed feet.

Moon

sits down at the end of the day,
pulls on its boots & zips up its jacket

to meet the dark in the bar, shouts
the first round then slags off the sun,

downs whiskies, sings songs, flirts
with some stars, any damn thing

to help it forget its gradually leaving

Charlie's room

By night my nephew's an astronaut,
sleeps in a space suit

at the base of a rocket trailblazing
a wall like a promise. The solar

system's strung out across the other,
quiet, in perfect proportion,

where he calculates stars, the purpose
of planets, why the moon is moving

away. Pluto sulks in the corner,
should never have been included

he tells me. The remaining walls are sky
blue. I buy him a second Earth

to project on the ceiling, signposting
home as he wakes.

ice cream 'n' tar

—how fast the summers go / they used to seem endless / when
the ice cream van with its music-box music brought us running,

our pockets full of pence, handing them over in sweaty fists to cool
palms with ice lollies / when we knocked on doors to ask friends

out to play, tag-chasing, bike-racing, anything to spend the energy
we had / when we kicked a ball with care, Mr Wilson's front garden

the goal we tried not to score, a weeping rose, a broken branch
rained down his wrath as we tried to look sorry / when being girl

or boy never mattered, chasing gnat clouds bare-skinned under
naked skies / when the light refused to leave, argued with the moon

as it appeared like a smirk to see who could last longer / when we
picked tar from our sandals after new road had been laid, careful

not to get it on our clothes because it was *a bugger to get off* / and
when school loomed closer, we played harder, ran faster—

Snow

One day, not far from now, children will ask what snow is.
It got knee-deep when I was young.

Drifts banked against doors and windows, schools closed.
Late afternoon on Sundays,

my brother and I would listen to the radio praying to hear
ours listed, high-fiving when we did.

We could be cut off for days staying with nan in the country,
the lane a blanket too thick to pull back,

outside muffled, electricity stilled. Our only heating came from
the fires she built in a room we rarely left,

except to make snowmen and pelt each other with balls
of it so it coated our gloves like icing.

These days, there is barely a sprinkle. It glitters, as if
to help us remember.

The tap

is one of those push down ones but it's broken
because someone's twisted
the top off so there's nothing to push down
and as the water's gushing
out into the cracked enamel sink and I'm thinking
what a waste this is a whale
plops out and starts singing followed by some fish
and a turtle who tells me
about the creatures we'll meet when everything's
flowed over and as I watch
them swimming and spinning I turn the tap off
at the mains because
we're not quite
ready yet.

A burning world

The fire spread at 60km an hour. We knew we'd have to evacuate, but thought we had more time. When it came, the whole mountain seemed to explode.

It was a land-eating monster, the noise was unbelievable. We've got friends who ran through firewalls. My brother had a bull killed sitting upright. It was instantly cooked, mummified.

I was stunned when we drove back. You hold out that tiny bit of hope, just maybe, there's something. But it was all gone, as if we'd never been here. I don't have one photo to show them what their grandmother looked like.

I've not seen my husband cry like this. For me, it comes in waves. I call myself a fire refugee, it's as if there's been a war.

There has to be some kind of transformation in the way we govern. I wish the people in power would listen. We've got to stop being such consumers. It's been a lesson for me, not to get attached to things.

Sourced from 'We've pissed mother nature off, big time: the people coming home after Australia's fires,' The Guardian, February 2020.

Silver spoons

I plant another succulent in our reluctant garden.
Cuttings can root anywhere, the same as geraniums

>	like my nan taught me, *as long as you leave enough
>	and the cut's alive* she said. She loved her plants,

>	took my arm to show me what's new, what's thriving,
>	what needs a little help. She snipped candy-sweet

>	roses and wrapped them in wet paper so I could
>	take them home. She had fuchsias tumbling from

>	baskets like waterfalls and sowed wild poppies
>	from seed, told me a hydrangea's colour depends

>	on where its feet stand. She bloomed delicate pinks,
>	potted happy-faced pansies, kept a buddleia blazing

with bees. Only succulents last here and I'm grateful
for their variety, careful to mix shapes, colour and size.

This one has spoon-shaped leaves, grows tall and silver,
like winters did.

Earth turn

When the woman sitting next to me points
out the beautiful sunset
(and indeed it is beautiful with the sky alight
over the steely-blue sea)
I want to correct her by saying it's actually
a beautiful earth turn because
the sun doesn't move we do and although
our home is doing all the work
we behave as if we're renting it and have
all the time in the world
to start the repairs but instead I cut a piece
of the grilled fish
on my plate then dip it in tartar sauce.

M. Nature Comes Home

Answer the door promptly when she knocks.
Invite her in to sit a while.
Make her some tea and note how she's aged—her thin hair,
her drawn face, how much smaller she seems—but don't mention it.
Offer to rub her feet while she sips a cup of camomile.
Talk to fill the silence.
Ask her how she's been, if she's whipped up any devastating storms
lately, where her last fire/flood/drought was.
Try not to notice the way she stares at you, how her mouth is tight,
her dark eyes ablaze despite her winter.
And try not to notice your tremble, which starts in your head
and swiftly spreads as though you're her next disaster.
Find your cheeks are wet, your mouth is dry, that you can't
quiet your heart.
Feel her reach inside you, rip through your arrogance, your empty
sorrys, what you said you would do and did not, until
you're a snivelling, snot-caked mess.
Know then, like lightning, how she wishes she was no mother at all.

Sorry

I step into the night where colour is sleeping.
Cold air fills my lungs like a clean fresh start.
Stars splinter the sky and the dunes swim
in moon. The quiet is ice-like, the still like glass.

As I squat to empty my bladder, I think how
insignificant we are, how on the infinite line
of time, we are just a pulse, a beat without heart,
how something so small can cause so much

damage, how very sorry we are.

An Evening with the Legendary Ms. Snow

(transcript from the archives of last recorded appearance)

Host (H): Welcome welcome, so good to see you again, it's been a while!

Ms. Snow (MS): Yes, I think the last time we met was seven years ago, when you asked me if I could fall for you *(beams, as if the moon's appeared from behind a cloud to illuminate a garden under a blanket of snow)*

(audience gasps)

H: Oh yes! And I seem to recall you didn't, much to my dismay, but you did let me kiss you...

MS: I did, yes, briefly, didn't want you catching a cold *(shivers, a sound reminiscent of sleigh bells in the snow)*

(audience laughs)

H: You've had a long and varied career. Let's take a look at some of your most memorable roles.

(cut to scenes of an avalanche, a snowball fight, white-capped mountains, a blizzard)

H: If you had to choose, which one was your favourite role?

MS: Oh, in the snowball fight for sure, hearing the children squealing with joy and having so much fun was really quite special *(recalls the joy and is momentarily stilled, like catching a falling flake of snow)*

H: And which would you say was your most challenging role?

MS: That would definitely have to be the avalanche. I spent months building myself up for that. I even had a personal trainer who helped me make the most of myself *(makes a sweeping gesture, scattering diamond-like bits of snow)*

H: Now I'm not one to gossip, but there have been rumours you've had a little work done recently. Care to share among friends?

MS: Hmmm, well, I won't lie, most of what you see here today is artificial. Trying to stay fresh these days is difficult to say the least *(flashes a blinding smile, like the morning sun finding an overnight drift of snow)*

H: So, you've a new book coming out, *Another Way to Be*, can you tell us a bit about it?

MS: In this world you need to be flexible, able to adapt to constant change quickly. One such way is by exploring other forms of yourself, so for example, I could morph into a patch of black ice on a road or become the mud-stained sludge at the end of winter. There are so many possibilities if you have the desire to keep going, to keep reinventing yourself *(induces a reverie, as if being the first to footprint a fresh fall of snow)*

H: Well, we've nearly run out of time as we don't want to keep you for long. Any parting words?

MS: Keep hold of what you have because one day, there may be nothing to hold *(glitters, like the ice buried in the deep heart of snow)*

(audience sighs)

H: Wise words indeed. It's been an absolute pleasure as always. Don't leave it so long next time!

MS: That's not really up to me, is it? *(winks at the audience then exits the stage, leaving a trail of melting snow)*

(audience whoops and whistles, as if trying to find something lost)

Ladybirds

I try to call you every three weeks to conjure you again.
Today's a good day, with your morning and my evening,

we span the in-between. You ask about me—
how I've been, my husband, my work—and I share

like this is routine. I reciprocate, mention your heatwave
blazing across our wintered news. You say it's been hot

but not a patch on the summer after I was born,
the hottest on record and when the ladybirds came.

You tell me again how you didn't know what to do
with me, tried to keep me cool by putting my pram

in the shade veiled in white cotton. I try to picture you
cooing and fanning to keep me appeased and can't.

Instead, I see a rippling swathe of ladybirds, a delicate
sea of red, lifting their skirts for any promise of breeze.

Coffin Bay

Crayfish, pilchards,
ocean jackets and sharks

Octopus, sea urchins,
sea snails and scallops

Sand crabs, abalone,
garfish and whiting

Shush
the oysters are sleeping.

Barrier Reef

(formerly Great)

The map is neatly new. The paper, parchment. An artist's impression. Picture book perfect. *Not to be used as a navigational aid.* I travel the length of Queensland in seconds. Swathes of thick green meet powder blue. A ribbon of colour ghosts its edge with bursts of pink and yellow, orange and purple. Coral before the climate effect. And there are big fish and small, jellied and finned. Black lines trailing them. As if that's what will follow. A snake slithers from a spidering sun. A turtle tracks the Tropic of Capricorn. Islands in between are barely visible. Hinchinbrook, Magnetic, Whitsunday. Beads along the coast's throat. Gateways to reef. What is the language here? How many Aboriginal ones are still spoken? Falling on closed ears. In a place that's screaming.

Every second counts

I sip takeaway tea from a closing café
as another species disappears.
It's overfull, burns my fingers.

I remove the plastic lid to let it cool,
bits of which will be found in a marine
mammal's stomach.

I think of our cat while a forest is flattened,
wonder how she's doing at home,
if she's missing outside.

As an ice shelf calves into the sea,
I check my phone
for tomorrow's weather.

Small beginnings

I search bread bin to replace one rusting,
as if it houses damp not oven-baked goods.
Infinite choices on endless pages. One catches
my eye in oat-milk with a bamboo lid that doubles

as a cutting board. I browse the site, find a matching
compost bin. I put both in my cart, with organic
mesh produce bags, compostable wrap,
washable dish cloths, reusable baking paper

and recyclable food pouches, eager to keep plastic
unmade, ignoring the footprint delivery will make.
I'm welcomed on the start of my sustainable journey
with a free sprouting jar, imagine small beginnings.

Turning

I meet Dark at the wrong time. He tells me
                     I'm late as he lights another star
    like a cigarette. I take a seat under
the moon he's leaning over. *So how much*
          do you know he asks, cocking his head further
into shadow. I feel the moon hold
    its breath, the ice of it lifting. *Probably more*
            than I should I reply,
tracking the path of a comet as it blazes through the room.
       Then you know how this ends
              Dark says, as he leans
forward to stroke the silver in my hair. I pull
    away to the moon
but he's now holding my chin, looming like
        a distant relative. Then, without
    warning, he brings out the world from his pocket,
                uncurls my clammy hand
to place it in my palm. Its greens and blues
    are not as green and blue and there's a sense
                  of falling. As Dark sits
back and stretches his legs, I try my best
        to keep it turning.

When the sky falls

You are human only
made of dead stars and space
and planet leftovers
spinning and living in your sliver of time
bound to the place that's birthed you
to return your borrowed bones.

I terror your nights
twist your hands like a lover
hellbent on revenge
and as you fight with your fightless body
cry for the voice that's fled your throat
I wonder at the meaning of you.

Crow

the black gloss
of his coat flashes
     iridescent blue
          his eyes are
               bottomless knots
                of things he can't
        unsee and in
     his mouth a tangle
of sound unravels
when he calls

primordial

it's out there beyond our vision
tracks us by the width of day
measure of moon
the space in between
notes how we work our land our stock our time
slick in our sweat & grease & snot

                                        it puts the cold in our hearts
                                            & the rocks in our blood
                            makes each thud an unwanted thing
                                  it compels us to undo our doing
                leave our fear in our boots for the dogs to mind
                                  it waits as we turn wild with waiting

then when night is punctured with eyes
& we've plundered ourselves
it calls to the dark in us
where shadows have breath & bone
& with one swift move
brings the absence of everything

The Ministers

The Minster for Drought submits a proposal. *Due to the severity of the current situation, I propose a ban on external H_2O use, worldwide, with immediate effect.*

The Minister for Green Grass objects.

The Minister for the Sun supports his objection, stating he cannot sustain the portfolio of his colleague alone.

The Minister for Drought relents, caveats his proposal with *on grass excepted*.

The Minister for Fresh Air releases an audible sigh.

The Minister for Blue Sky clears his throat.

The Minster for Wind and the Minister for Solar exchange looks, having united since the Minister for Mining resigned.

The Minister for the Moon appears, he is rarely in attendance.

The Minister for Tides rises to his feet and continues to rise, pressure builds.

Order, order! cries the Minister for Earth, struggling to be heard.

After the Anthropocene

***Homo sapiens
mid-week special***

Best in pots to prevent spread.

                                      Does not mix well. Plant like with like.

        Different varieties available – frost-hardy, coastal, mature, baby.

Not drought tolerant. Water generously.

                                      Thrives in part sun and part shade.

Prone to disease. Treat with care.

              Big hit during summer when smothered in colour.

                                              Cut down to size.
For ornamental purposes only.

    A lovely addition to any garden. A vintage style for any home.

Sourced from plant labels.

Epilogue

Rot

I don't understand people with fruit trees
who don't pick the fruit.

        Why have them
        if you're just going to let their little gifts rot?

The shriek of birds from the branches
doesn't convince me.

        Maybe they don't like fruit
        or they're renting and couldn't care less.

I pick up dying peaches
pocket-sized planets slowly wasting.

        But why not save the fruit
        and leave it for others to enjoy?

Untouched ones hanging catch my eye
their skins signalling sweetness

        like a promise of hope

Selected Poetry Titles Published by SurVision Books

Seeds of Gravity: An Anthology of Contemporary Surrealist Poetry from Ireland
Edited by Anatoly Kudryavitsky
ISBN 978-1-912963-18-8

Invasion: An Anthology of Ukrainian Poetry about the War
Edited by Tony Kitt
ISBN 978-1-912963-32-4

Noelle Kocot. *Humanity*
(New Poetics: USA)
ISBN 978-1-9995903-0-7

Marc Vincenz. *Einstein Fledermaus*
(New Poetics: USA)
ISBN 978-1-912963-20-1

Helen Ivory. *Maps of the Abandoned City*
(New Poetics: England)
ISBN 978-1-912963-04-1

Tony Kitt. *The Magic Phlute*
(New Poetics: Ireland)
ISBN 978-1-912963-08-9

Clayre Benzadón. *Liminal Zenith*
(New Poetics: USA)
ISBN 978-1-912963-11-9

Thomas Townsley. *Tangent of Ardency*
(New Poetics: USA)
ISBN 978-1-912963-15-7

Mikko Harvey & Jake Bauer. *Idaho Falls*
(Winner of James Tate Poetry Prize 2018)
ISBN 978-1-912963-02-7

Alison Dunhill. *As Pure as Coal Dust*
(Winner of James Tate Poetry Prize 2020)
ISBN 978-1-912963-23-2

Charles Borkhuis. *Spontaneous Combustion*
(Winner of James Tate Poetry Prize 2021)
ISBN 978-1-912963-30-0

Noah Falck and Matt McBride. *Prerecorded Weather*
(Winner of James Tate Poetry Prize 2022)
ISBN 978-1-912963-39-3

Michael Zeferino Spring. *Kahlo's Window*
(Winner of James Tate Poetry Prize 2022)
ISBN 978-1-912963-40-9

Dominique Hecq. *Endgame with No Ending*
(Winner of James Tate Poetry Prize 2022)
ISBN 978-1-912963-42-3

Ciaran O'Driscoll. *Angel Hour*
ISBN 978-1-912963-27-0

George Kalamaras. *That Moment of Wept*
ISBN 978-1-9995903-7-6

George Kalamaras. *Through the Silk-Heavy Rains*
ISBN 978-1-912963-28-7

Order our books from http://survisionmagazine.com/bookshop.htm

www.ingramcontent.com/pod-product-compliance
Lightning Source LLC
Chambersburg PA
CBHW061315040426
42444CB00010B/2658